ЕРЬ БУ=РҐЬ.

G

Almost at the foot of St Isaac's, on a square enclosed on two sides by calm, clear-cut, majestic buildings of the Admiralty and the Synod and Senate and washed on the third by the regal Neva, stands the monument set up by Catherine II to Peter the Great: *Petro Primo Catharina Secunda*. If anybody happens to be near it on a foul autumn evening, when the sky turned to chaos comes close to the earth and fills it with its commotion, the river constricted in granite groans and tosses, sudden gusts of wind set street-lamps swinging and their juddering light makes the surrounding buildings quiver — he should take a look in a moment like that at the Bronze Horseman, at that fire transformed to copper with sharply-drawn, powerful forms. What a force he will sense — a passionate, impetuous force summoning to the unknown. What a great sweeping gesture, evoking the alarmed question: what's to come, what's ahead? Victory or failure and death? The Bronze Horseman is the spirit of Petersburg.

Nikolai Antsiferov,
The Soul of Petersburg, 1922

AURORA ART PUBLISHERS · ST PETERSBURG

Saint Petersburg

*Founded
on 27 May 1703*

SAINT PETERSBURG

In 2003 St Petersburg will be three hundred years old. Compared with the hoary stones of Paris, Kiev or Cologne, the city on the Neva really does seem a youngster. There is nothing ancient about it; it never knew the Middle Ages.

It did not just appear — it was conceived by Peter the Great as "a window to Europe", as the capital of a "young Russia".

It was constructed according to a rational plan; its architects, as a rule, designed not simply buildings, but whole ensembles; the streets were wide and straight, the squares unusually spacious. But there are few cities in the world so "fantastical" (Dostoyevsky), irrational, uneasy and inexplicable, grand and mysterious, so full of great shades and memories, as St Petersburg at less than three hundred years old.

Following its foundation in 1703, it was the capital for a little over two centuries (1712 — 1918). St Petersburg has come to share the distinctive and proud lot of "second cities" around the world, such as Florence, Munich, New York or Seville, which, while yielding precedence to the capital, have preserved their fame and importance even after losing their official status.

But St Petersburg has one important peculiarity: not only was it a capital — it was built as a capital. This is the source of the sweep and grandeur which has caused such delight, the source too of the austere officialism, even coldness which has so often been cursed.

Indeed, there were many whom the city delighted, calling it the Venice of the North, the Northern Palmyra. It inspired perhaps the best of Pushkin's verses. The city gave birth to its own literature, its own mythology, and, of course, its own art. Yet the culture associated with St Petersburg always contained and still contains within it a certain uneasiness. Admiration for the city was tinged with a hint of sadness. Its "austere, elegant appearance" (Pushkin) impresses with its stern refinement, but not with its warmth. It does not gladden the heart, does not promise cosiness, but generously gratifies the human passion for beauty and harmony. A particular, peculiar city!

The observer with an inclination to seek out in St Petersburg the face of its past will easily come upon views which recall the different pages in its history to life. But to do so requires imagination and a certain degree of knowledge.

As they appear today the streets and squares of central St Petersburg, its embankments, bridges, monuments and famous palaces are reminders primarily of the last decades of the eighteenth century and of the nineteenth. The elegant, finely-planned ensembles, colonnades in the opulent Baroque or more austere Classical style, bronze sculptures on granite façades, the five- or six-storey buildings along Nevsky Prospekt and the agglomerations of tenement houses in the less stylish areas, where one cannot help but remember Dostoyevsky — this is a far cry from the St Petersburg which Peter I dreamt of and which — during his own reign and the years which followed — at least in part reflected his dreams. That city, the "Petrine" one, was squat and low. The first stone buildings seemed smaller still on the banks of the wide river, and only the rare towers topped with spires and the flagstaffs with their flags fluttering in the Baltic wind relieved the monotonous look of the capital on the Neva. To some extent this scene recreated the appearance of Peter's beloved Holland, although the majestic Neva and the already-foreseeable future scale of the city belonged to another world and another time. In addition, Peter, who dreamt too of Italy, proposed constructing a large number of canals like in Venice; and Domenico Trezzini, the architect who constructed the most important projects in the young capital, was an Italian by birth. It was not for nothing that the term "Petrine Baroque" was later coined to define the unusual architecture of the first quarter of the eighteenth century, in which simple-planned buildings were enlivened by not over-rich Baroque decoration. Such were the SS Peter and Paul Cathedral in the fortress of the same name — the starting place for the construction of the city, the building of the Twelve Collegia or ministries, and the first dwelling-houses. The buildings were created in brick, plastered and painted different colours; even in the time of the Baroque and Classical styles they were not, as, say, in Paris, made of stone or given the colour of stone. Yellow, azure, turquoise and terracotta façades, rhythmically divided by white

PORTRAIT OF PETER THE GREAT. 1717
By Jean-Marc Nattier

columns and pilasters with dark-ochre, and sometimes even gilded, capitals, endow St Petersburg with an absolutely distinctive range of colours and bring life to streets that do not see the sun that often, being more accustomed to gloom, rain and fog.

Peter himself never saw dreams come true, but the Emperor's idea of the appearance of the city was brought into life by architects who began working to his commission. The three component parts of St Petersburg were the Peter and Paul Fortress on Zayachy (Hare) Island, Vasilyevsky (Basil's) Island to the right of the main channel of the Neva, and the Moscow Side (with the enormous shipyard of the Admiralty, which gave it its second name) on the left bank. Three radial streets extending south and west of the Admiralty — chief among them, the "Nevsky perspective road" — became the most important thoroughfares in the city. The city turned its face to the immense, chilly river, still not crossed by bridges. Ships from various corners of the globe sailed high up the Neva, their masts and flags adding, as it were, to the number of towers and spires on the banks...

The heart of the city has, in essence, remained the same. As before slender spires pierce the grey sky; the same trident of main streets still cuts across the city. But much had already begun to change in the first decades after Peter's death. The dryish manner of Domenico Trezzini was succeeded by the opulent fantasy of Francesco Bartolommeo Rastrelli. The grand splendour of the Baroque decoration used on the incomparable Winter Palace — the royal residence on the bank of the Neva, and on the palaces built for Count Mikhail Vorontsov on Sadovaya Street and Count Sergei Stroganov on Nevsky Prospekt together with the refined elegance of Smolny Cathedral gave the city a hitherto unknown stylishness and the true lustre of a capital. Incidentally, these were more like a sprinkling of magical dust, precious insertions into the map of the city, rather than component parts of architectural ensembles.

The turn of the nineteenth century became to a significant degree a turning point for the appearance of the city. Classicism with its striving after triumphal monumentalism, strict architectonics and the ensemble gave the city back the unity Peter had conceived. Adrian Zakharov's reconstruction of the Admiralty with a spire raising the gilded sailing-ship weather-vane to a height of seventy-two metres — a building full of dignity and true grandeur — determined, as it were, the scale and

MONUMENT TO PETER THE GREAT. 1821—22. By Andrei Martynov

sweep of construction in the capital. With a semicircle of buildings joined by a tremendous arch Carlo Rossi closed off the square in front of the Winter Palace. He created the ensembles on Mikhailovskaya, Alexandrinskaya and Senatskaya Squares to give the centre of the city a regal completeness. Earlier still, Andrey Voronikhin had erected the Cathedral of Our Lady of Kazan with its open colonnades facing Nevsky Prospekt. St Isaac's Cathedral — the tallest building in the city — and the Alexander Column in front of the Winter Palace, both the creations of Auguste Montferrand, to a large extent summed up the construction work of the nineteenth century. Over the course of the century a wonderful capital had appeared, created in one breath, so to speak; a spacious and harmonious city, surprising the visitor with its rare unity and majestic calm.

Bronze tsars and generals stand rigid on their granite pediments, frozen too is Etienne Maurice Falconet's celebrated "Bronze Horseman", that monument to an emperor who "made Russia rear up" (Pushkin). The city is populated and animated by superb works of sculpture, the icing on the cake of the architectural ensembles. The gilded spires echo each other — the SS Peter and Paul Cathedral and St Isaac's, the Admiralty and St Michael's (Engineers') Castle. Stone embankments with architecturally surprising landings adorn the Neva. Finally, in place of the single pontoon bridge, huge drawbridges appear.

Since the middle of the last century the look of the city has altered little. The countless apartment houses (among which there are many architectural masterpieces, altough still more are utterly mediocre), the elegant, and not ineffective, architecture of the style that has become known as eclectic, and even the cultivated and exquisite refinement of the brilliant St Petersburg *art nouveau* could no longer principally change the face of the city, but only made St Petersburg more heterogeneous and interesting.

But not a single excursus into the history of the city's architecture can replace the visual impression of that divine unity of buildings and ensembles constructed at different times, that harmony of stones and water, that "indivisible dissimilarity" which make Nevsky Prospekt and the Petrograd Side, Kolomna and the Summer Gardens, and many other places in St Petersburg both unlike each other and at the same time intrinsically part of the city.

There is the city celebrated by Pushkin in his verse — the "beauty and wonder of the northern lands" — which can amaze a person standing in its very centre, on Palace Bridge, say. From there you can see the elegant pavilions of the Admiralty and the row of buildings that make up the Hermitage from the Winter Palace to the Winter Canal (across which Giacomo Quarenghi threw an arch inimitable in its stern finesse), the steep bridges over the canals, the Peter and Paul Fortress and the Spit of Vasilyevsky Island, where the majestic building of the Exchange stands flanked by the mighty Rostral Columns.

There is amazing Nevsky Prospekt — "St Petersburg's common line of communication... Almighty Nevsky Prospekt..." (Gogol) — in which you can read the history of the city and discern its changeable face. The street is straight and wide, every now and again revealing views of enchantingly beautiful ensembles — the Mikhailovsky Palace or the Alexandrinsky Theatre, so utterly harmonious that at times they seem to be stage decorations. Nevsky is crossed by two small rivers and a canal, their unexpected sharp turns pleasantly relieving the undeviating straightness of the street. And if you turn to walk along one of their narrow embankments, you find yourself in a completely different world, a world of quiet, narrow water, hanging trees and indispensable little bridges, sometimes decorated with eccentric sculptures, old lamps and railings. You can follow them to the Neva, but if you go deeper into the city, you find yourself in quiet districts which have little attraction, but possess their own lyricism nonetheless — perhaps in Kolomna, the sad back-of-beyond as far as St Petersburg is concerned, home to the heroes of Gogol, Pushkin and Dostoyevsky.

On Vasilyevsky Island, right on the bank of the Neva, two ancient stone sphinxes brought from Egypt stand rigidly. Spreading out behind the façades of the "Academy of the Three Most Noble Arts" is the most "geometric" part of the city, regularly laid out for canals that after only a few years were filled in to become streets yet are still known as "lines" and distinguished only by numbers.

Scarcely inferior to Nevsky is Kamennoostrovsky Prospekt which runs through the whole Petrograd Side district so as to become airborne on the most beautiful of the city's bridges — Trinity Bridge decorated in a deliberate, even excessive display of refinement with railings and lamps in the purest *art nouveau* style, a bridge on which even the masts supporting the wires for the trams have been designed with an especial neurotic subtlety.

And further, on the opposite bank, is the tremendous esplanade of the Field of Mars and the green massif of the Summer Gardens with their legendary railing, perhaps the most beautiful in the world.

Every city has a historical and moral drama of its own. The beauty of St Petersburg, celebrated by many poets, delights the eye, but rarely warms the heart. The antithesis between Muscovite patriarchal cosiness and the cool elegance of St Petersburg has become a truism, but there is undoubtedly a grain of truth in such a view of things. A strange "poetry of bureaucracy" (are there any other cities like this in the world?) found sublime artistic expression in St Petersburg. Order, pedantry, raised to the level of an aesthetic category, introduced a particular, oppressive logic into its architecture. The city is hardly likely to produce surprises: there is not a single hillock, not one gully, and there are but few crooked sreets. St Petersburg was born to become the capital of a vast empire. Its life, brief by historical standards, has been rich in political tragedies. Here the Russian history of modern times was determined. The streets ran red with the blood of rulers and their subjects. It was here that the revolution took place which shook the world — probably the greatest social drama of the century. Happily, misfortunes, although they age a city, at times also bring it an especial, wise kind of beauty and fill its streets with memories which evoke whole chains of associations.

It is only natural that such a city should have produced its own legends, its own mythology. The streets seem peopled not only by the ghosts of great writers, but by their characters as well, characters who simply could not exist, nor even appear in any other city — the creations of Pushkin and Gogol, Dostoyevsky and Blok. They were born of the very atmosphere of the city, where "everything is deceit, everything a dream, nothing what it seems" (Gogol), where the traditional Russian character entered into dramatic conflict with a capital conceived by Peter in the European manner. And in the icy setting of St Petersburg human passions grew especially ardent and poignant. Penetrating through the "window to Europe" which Peter I had cut out, the Hoffmannesque grotesque of the world beyond took on a unique Russian individuality in Petersburg culture.

Dostoyevsky wrote that Russian man "had already acquired the capacity to become most Russian only when he was at his most European". Possibly, precisely here, in St Petersburg, Russian architecture and urbanism, having come directly into contact with the western cultural tradition and made it an integral part of the city's intellectual and artistic life, created something wholly original, the like of which will scarcely be found — a great city on the frontier of West and East, a city attractive to the Russian and the Western European alike and for both of them something surprising, "fantastical".

So much has already been written about how beautiful St Petersburg is. Its celebrated white nights which do not permit "the shadow of night onto the golden skies" (Pushkin), when the city is transformed into an utterly unreal spectacle; the hoar-frost which covers the granite of the columns in dimly glittering silver when the temperature rises in winter; the rains and mists of autumn which so become the city — all of these have been described many times by the best writers in Russia.

An astonishing city — capable of making even its tragedies a source of poetic revelation! The devastating flood of 1824 was a considerable part of the inspiration behind Pushkin's poem *The Bronze Horseman*; even the 900-day siege during World War II evoked no small number of verses and paintings. Indeed, the whole dramatic history of St Petersburg, which has experienced not only the bloody toppling of regimes, not only periods of social stagnation, but even the loss of its own name, has invariably and consistently been perceived through the mirror of art. And that is how St Petersburg was conceived — to be the visible expression of the New Russia, the touchstone of taste, harmony, reason... of all that which the busy pedestrian always senses, walking — even for the hundredth time — through the streets of St Petersburg.

Mikhail Guerman

...Nowhere did the white nights gain such control over minds, become so full of meaning, so saturated with poetry, as there in Petersburg, there by the waters of the Neva. I think that Peter himself, when he founded his Petersburg in May, was enchanted by one such white night, something unknown in the central part of Russia.

Alexander Benois,
My Memoirs, 1934

...You will scarcely find another city in the world which demanded greater sacrifices at its birth than the Palmyra of the North. Petersburg truly is a city built on human bones. The fogs and marshes from which the city appeared testify to the Trojan labour which had to be carried out in order to construct — on unstable soil, seemingly woven out of the mists — this "Paradise". Everything here speaks of a great struggle with nature. Everything here is "in defiance of the elements". In nature nothing was permanent, sharply drawn or proudly pointing skyward; everything clung to the earth as if waiting resignedly for the waters to close over this forlorn land. And the city was created like an antithesis of the surrounding nature, or a challenge to it. Let "chaos be stirring" beneath its squares, streets and canals — the city itself is all calm straight lines, hard, firm stone, precise, strict and regal with its golden spires serenely rising to the heavens.

Nikolai Antsiferov,
The Soul of Petersburg, 1922

3

4

Previous page:

1 Ioannovsky (St John's) Bridge at the
entrance to the Peter and Paul Fortress

2 The Royal Doors of the iconostasis in the
SS Peter and Paul Cathedral

On 27 May 1703 — the date considered to be
the birthday of the city — the Peter and Paul
Fortress was begun at the command and to the
plan of Peter the Great on Zayachy (Hare)
Island. Between 1705 and 1734 the architect
Domenico Trezzini was in charge of work here.
Standing on Cathedral Square is the SS Peter
and Paul Cathedral — a piece of architecture
in the Petrine Baroque style which Trezzini built
in 1712 — 33. Its dominant feature is the
multi-tiered bell-tower topped by a gilded spire
and a weather-vane in the form of a flying angel
(its total height is 122.5 metres). The
cathedral became the burial place of the
Russian emperors from Peter the Great onwards.
It contains a magnificent carved wooden
iconostasis created in 1722 — 26 by I. Zarudny

3

5

6

7

8

10

in the traditions of the European Baroque. Close by the cathedral is the boathouse, built in 1761 − 62 by A. Vist to keep the "grandfather of the Russian fleet" − the boat in which Peter the Great had learnt to sail.

3   SS Peter and Paul Cathedral and the Boathouse on Cathedral Square

4   The Emperor's Throne in the SS Peter and Paul Cathedral

5   The Vasilyevskiye Gate

6   Detail of the iconostasis in the SS Peter and Paul Cathedral

7   Archangel Michael. Detail of the Royal Doors

8   View of the Peter and Paul Fortress from Palace Embankment

9   The Peter Gate

10   Tombs of Peter the Great, Catherine I, Anne I, Peter III and Catherine II

9

11

12

11　View of the Winter Palace, Admiralty,
St Isaac's Cathedral and the Spit of Vasilyevsky
Island

12　View of the Academy of Sciences
(1783 — 85, architect Giacomo Quarenghi)
and the *Kunstkammer* (1718 — 34, architect
Mikhail Zemtsov, Georg Johann Mattarnovi,
Nikolaus Herbel and Gaetano Chiaveri;
1754 — 58, architect Savva Chevakinsky)
from Admiralty Embankment

13　Sculptural group on the pediment of the
Exchange building

14　The Exchange (Central Naval Museum).
1805 — 10. Architect Jean-François Thomas
de Thomon

13

14

15 The Pushkin House (Russian Academy of Sciences Institute of Russian Literature; the building of the former St Petersburg Customs House). 1829 — 31. Architect Giovanni Luchini

16 View of the Spit of Vasilyevsky Island (architect Jean-François Thomas de Thomon) from Palace Embankment

17 Rostral column on the Spit of Vasilyevsky Island (sculptures after models by I. Chamberlain and J. Thibault)

18 The Academy of Arts. 1764 — 88. Architects Alexander Kokorinov and Jean-Baptiste Vallin de la Mothe

Overleaf:

19 The Menshikov Palace from University Embankment

20 The inner courtyard

21, 22 The palace interiors

23 Monument to Peter the Great ("The Bronze Horseman"). 1774 — 78. Sculptor Etienne Maurice Falconet

24 View of Decembrists' Square from Admiralty Embankment

15

16

19

20

21

The Menshikov Palace is a fine example of the architecture of the Petrine Baroque. It was built in two stages, 1710 – 12 and 1713 – 27 (architects: Giovanni Fontana and Gottfried Schädel), for Prince Alexander Menshikov — the close friend and associate of Peter the Great. The façades with their simple finishing are typical for Petersburg architecture in the early eighteenth century. The relatively small and low rooms in the palace have large glazed windows and doors and are decorated with ceramic tiles, carved wooden panels, silks and paintings. Before the October Revolution of 1917 the building housed the First Cadet Corps; after it, the Military-Political College and other institutions. In 1967 the palace was given to the Hermitage department of early eighteenth-century Russian culture.

22

25

26

27

St Isaac's Cathedral, a great work of late Classical architecture, was the chief place of worship in St Petersburg before the October Revolution of 1917. The first wooden church on this site was founded in 1710 in honour of Peter the Great and named after Isaac of Dalmatia because Peter was born on that saint's feast-day (30 May O.S.). The cathedral we see today was built between 1818 and 1858 to the design of Auguste Montferrand and is one of the major achievements of Russian construction technique. The building is decorated with statues and high reliefs; the interior is finished with malachite, lapis lazuli, porphyry and various kinds of marble and adorned with mosaics, paintings, bronze and gilding.

St Isaac's Cathedral is an extremely important landmark in St Petersburg, determining together with the SS Peter and Paul Cathedral and the Admiralty the city's silhouette.

25, 28, 29   St Isaac's Cathedral

26   Central part of the iconostasis

27   Colonnade of the iconostasis

28

30

31

The Yusupov Palace was created in the
Classical style in the 1760s by the architect
Jean-Baptiste Vallin de la Mothe. In the second
half of the nineteenth century the interior of the
palace's private theatre was redecorated
in Baroque style by Ippolito Monighetti.
In 1830 the palace came into the possession of
Prince Nikolai Yusupov, one of the richest men
in Russia, and it remained with his descendants
until 1917. In the early hours of 17 December
1916 a group of conspirators including Felix
Yusupov, the son of the house (*see № 105*),
hoping to save the monarchy killed the royal
favourite Rasputin here in the palace.
Now the building functions as a Teachers'
Club. Today the palace theatre is once again
used for concerts and theatrical performances.

30   The Yusupov Palace

31   The puppeteer Vladimir Ordin

32   Scene from Tchaikovsky's ballet *Swan
Lake* in the Mariinsky Theatre

33   Interior of the Yusupov Palace theatre

34, 35   The building and auditorium of the
Mariinsky Theatre

32

33

36

37

38

The Mariinsky Opera and Ballet Theatre is one
of the largest and most important theatres in
Russia. Its history can be traced back to 1783.
Outstanding Russian singers, including the
great Chaliapin, sang in the opera company
here, performing works by Mussorgsky,
Rimsky-Korsakov, Tchaikovsky and others.
The ballet company of the Mariinsky Theatre —
the Kirov Ballet — is known throughout the
world and has undoubtedly had an influence
on many of the ballet schools of Europe and
America.

36, 37   Scenes from Tchaikovsky's opera *The
Queen of Spades* in the Mariinsky Theatre

38   *The Christmas Mystery* staged by the
Zazerkalye Theatre

39   Scene from Rimsky-Korsakov's opera *The
Maid of Pskov* in the Mariinsky Theatre

39

40

41

42

The Admiralty was constructed in 1806 – 23 by the architect Adrian Zakharov on the site of the Admiralty Shipyard founded in 1704 on the left bank of the Bolshaya (Greater) Neva and originally designed by Peter the Great. The Admiralty is a key architectural focus and the meeting-point of the three main streets in the city centre: Nevsky Prospekt, Voznesensky Prospekt and Gorokhovaya Street. The building is an outstanding example of Classicism, a brilliant synthesis of architecture and sculpture. The plastic decoration conveys the idea of Russia's might as a naval power. The spire on the central tower is crowned by a gilded weather-vane shaped like a sailing-ship, which has become a symbol of the city. In the nineteenth and twentieth centuries the building housed the Naval Ministry, the Naval Staff and other bodies, now it is the Higher Naval Engineering College.

40, 41   The Admiralty

42   One of the two pavilions of the Admiralty building facing the Neva

43   The Alexander Column (1830 — 34, architect Auguste Montferrand) on Palace Square

44

45

46

47

The Hermitage is one of the largest art museums in the world. It occupies five interconnected buildings on Palace Embankment and Millionnaya Street behind: the Winter Palace, the Small Hermitage, Old Hermitage, New Hermitage and Hermitage Theatre. The museum contains items of art produced by primitive cultures, others from the Classical world and from the East, ancient and modern, as well as paintings and graphic works by Western European artists and examples of decorative and applied art. The museum's exhibits are displayed in over 350 rooms.

The Winter Palace — a masterpiece of Baroque architecture — was built by Francesco Bartolommeo Rastrelli in 1754 — 62. Its façades look onto the Neva, the Admiralty and Palace Square. From the 1760s the palace was the residence of the Russian rulers and the venue for the emperors' grand public appearances, receptions, balls and other ceremonies.

The Jordan Staircase — the main one in the Winter Palace — gets its name from the fact that at Epiphany members of the imperial family and the senior clergy left the palace here to cross the embankment to a special pavilion known as a "Jordan" erected by the Neva for the traditional Orthodox ceremony of the Blessing of the Waters.

The New Hermitage faces Millionnaya Street. Its portico is supported by ten atlantes carved in granite by Alexander Terebenev.

The Winter Canal, dug out in 1718 — 19 from the Neva to the Moika River, now lies between the Old Hermitage and the Hermitage Theatre which are connected by a covered gallery.

44 — 47   The Winter Palace

48, 50   View of the Winter Canal

49   Portico of the New Hermitage

52

55

56

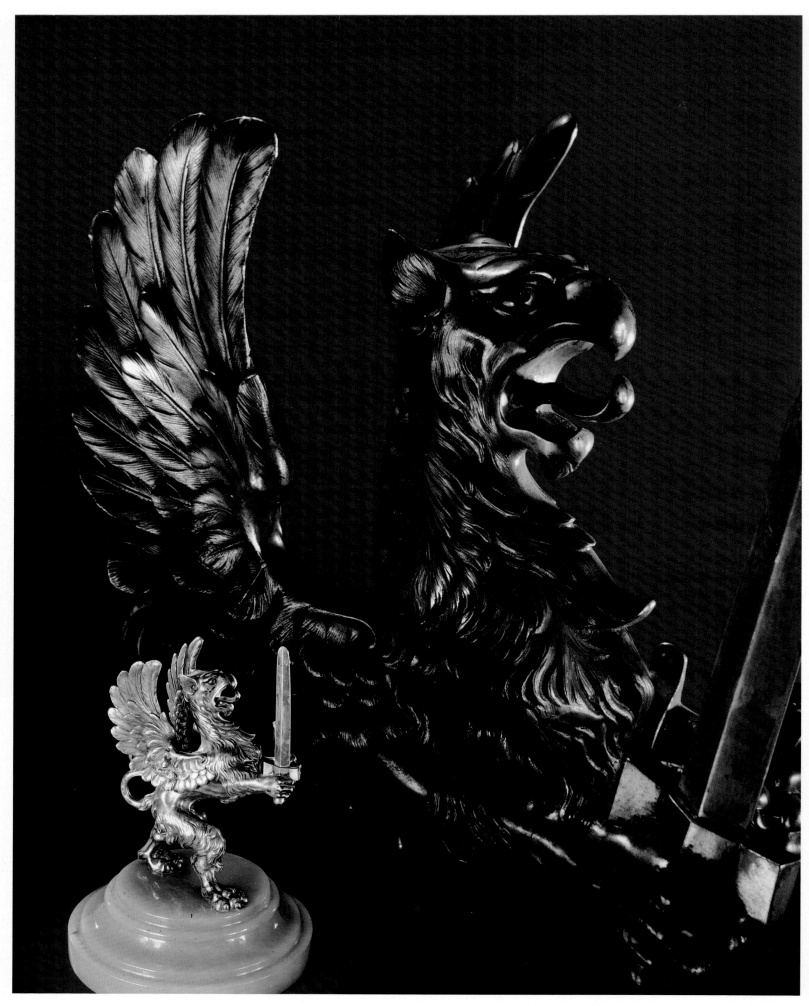

57   GRYPHON, THE COAT OF ARMS OF THE ROMANOV HOUSE. 1898
The Fabergé Company
The Hermitage Museum

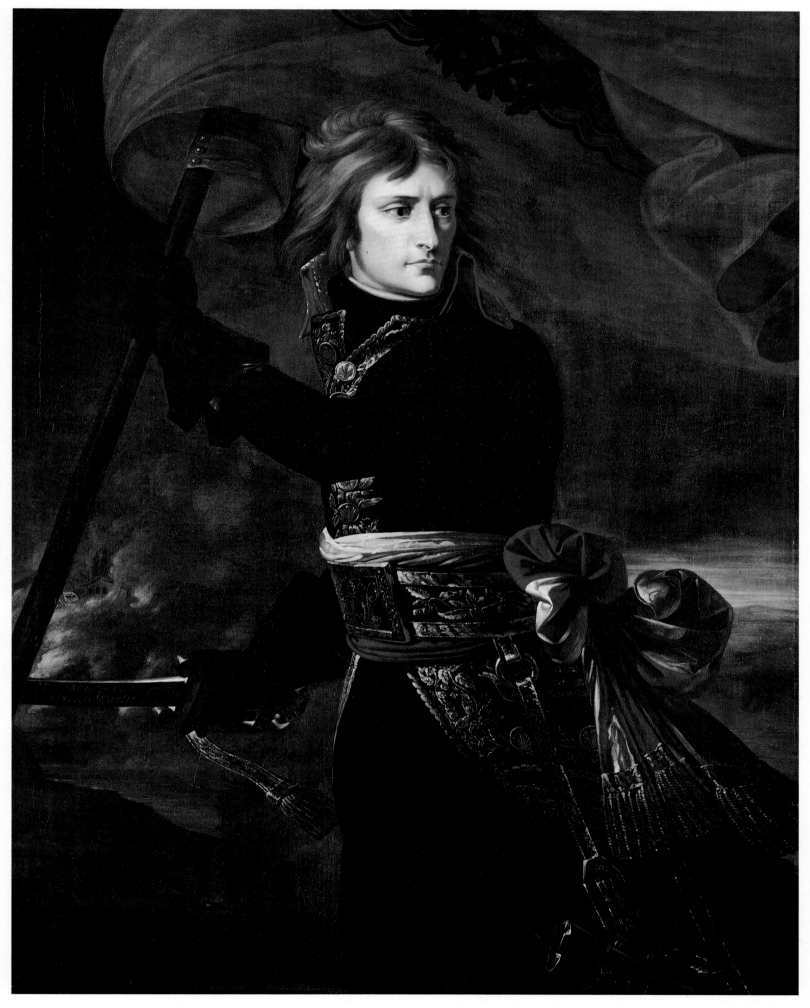

58   NAPOLEON ON THE ARCOLE BRIDGE. 1796/97
By Jean Antoine Gros
The Hermitage Museum

61

62

The Pushkin Memorial Flat is situated at number 12 on Moika Embankment. The great Russian poet lived here from the autumn of 1836. On 29 January 1837 Pushkin died in his study of a wound received in a duel with Georges d'Anthès.

63

The Summer Gardens were laid out in 1704 at the command of Peter the Great alongside his summer residence. They are located on the left bank of the Neva on an island formed by the Moika and Fontanka Rivers and the Swan Canal. The gardens were adorned with numerous statues, sculptural groups and busts (predominantly Italian work of the late seventeenth and early eighteenth centuries) and with fountains. Out of 250 sculptures, 89 still survive. From the middle of the eighteenth century the Summer Gardens were the place where the aristocracy went to stroll (ordinary people were not allowed in); in the early nineteenth century some of the alleys were converted to permit horseback riding.
The railings which separate the Summer Gardens from Neva embankment were set up in 1773 – 86 (architects: Georg Friedrich Velten, Piotr Yegorov and Timofei Nasonov). In 1839 a decorative vase made of pink porphyry which had been presented by the King of Sweden to Nicholas I was set up on the edge of the Carp Pond.

66   The railings of the Summer Gardens facing the Neva

67   The Summer Palace of Peter the Great

68   Monument to the fabulist Ivan Krylov. 1855. Sculptor Piotr Klodt

69   Central alley in the Summer Gardens

70

71

72

73

70   The Rossi Pavilion (Coffee House). 1826.
Architect Carlo Rossi

71   Vase of pink porphyry in the Summer
Gardens

72   The Dining Room in the Summer Palace

73   The Study in the Cabin of Peter the Great

74   *Peace and Abundance*. 1722. Sculptor
Pietro Baratta

75   The Summer Palace in winter

76   *Cupid and Psyche*. Late 17th century

74

The Mikhailovsky (St Michael) Castle was built in 1797 — 1800 by a great practitioner of the Classical style, Vincenzo Brenna. In 1800 Carlo Bartolommeo Rastrelli's equestrian statue of Peter the Great was set up in front of the building. The castle was constructed as a residence for Paul I (whose patron saint was the Archangel Michael), but the emperor was destined to live in it less than two months. On the night of 11 March 1801 he was murdered by conspirators in the state bed-chamber of the palace. In 1819 the castle was given over to the Chief Engineering College, hence its second name — the Engineers' Castle. Its pupils later included the writer Dostoyevsky.

77   The Mikhailovsky (St Michael) Castle from the Swan Canal

78, 80   The Mikhailovsky Castle

79   Monument to Peter the Great in front of the Mikhailovsky Castle

77

78

ПРАДѢДУ

ПРАВНУКЪ

1800

81

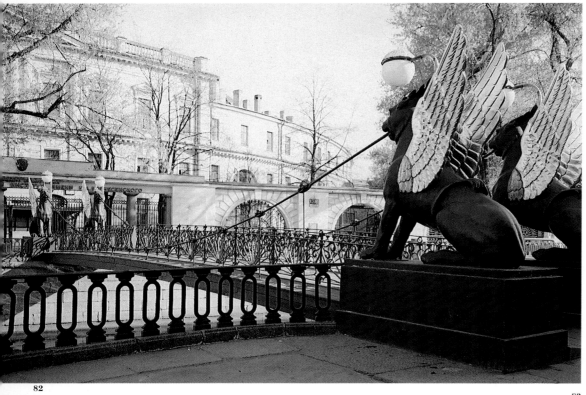

82

Bridges are an inseparable element in the architectural landscape of this "Northern Venice" washed by the waters of the Neva and transected by its many branches, smaller rivers and canals. In St Petersburg and the suburbs there are some 800 bridges. Something special is added to the feel of the city by the raising of the bridges across the Neva at night to allow large ships to pass up and down. This regular practice becomes a moving spectacle in the White Nights of June.

81   Lion Bridge over the Griboyedov Canal. 1825 — 26. Engineers G. Traitteur and V. Khristianovich

82   Bank Bridge over the Griboyedov Canal. 1825 — 26. Engineer G. Traitteur

83   Peter the Great Bridge across the Neva. 1908 — 11. Engineers G. Krivoshein, S. Bobrovsky and G. Perederiy

83

84

85

86

87

84   Laundry Bridge over the Fontanka River. 1766 — 69. Architects Ignazio Rossi and Timofei Nasonov

85   Anichkov Bridge over the Fontanka River. 1906 — 08. Engineers S. Bobrovsky, G. Krivoshein; architect Piotr Shchusev

86   Chernyshov Bridge over the Fontanka River. 1785 — 87. Engineer A. Viazemsky

87   Malo-Koniushenny and Theatre Bridges spanning the junction of the Moika River and the Griboyedov Canal. 1829 — 30. Engineers G. Traitteur and Ye. Adam

88   Trinity Bridge raised at night

89   Trinity Bridge. 1897 — 1903. Designed by the French Batignolle Company; built with a participation of Russian engineers

88

89

90

91

90   The Alexander Column and the General
Staff building (*right*; 1819 — 29, architect
Carlo Rossi) on Palace Square

91   Sculptural group on the arch of the
General Staff. Sculptors Stepan Pimenov and
Vasily Demuth-Malinovsky

92   The Cathedral of Our Lady of Kazan.
1801 — 11. Architect Andrei Voronikhin

93   Monument to Mikhail Kutuzov. 1837.
Sculptor Boris Orlovsky, architect Vasily
Stasov

94   Nevsky Prospekt

93

92

The Church of the Resurrection of Christ (or the "Saviour-on-the-Spilt-Blood") was built in 1883 – 1907 (architects: I. Makarov and A. Parland) as a memorial church on the spot where Emperor Alexander II was fatally wounded by revolutionary terrorists on 1 March 1881. The style of the building was inspired by Russian architecture of the sixteenth and seventeenth centuries. It employs, in particular, compositional devices first used in the creation of St Basil's Cathedral on Red Square in Moscow.

95   The Church of the Resurrection of Christ (the "Saviour-on-the-Spilt-Blood")

The Mikhailovsky Palace was constructed in 1819 – 25 in Classical style by Carlo Rossi to be the residence of Grand Duke Mikhail, the brother of Alexander I and Nicholas I. Between 1895 and 1898 it was converted to become the Emperor Alexander III Russian Museum, now simply the Russian Museum. In the early 1900s a wing was built to house the museum's ethnographic department, which later became independent (and is now the Russian Ethnographic Museum). Alongside the Tretyakov Gallery in Moscow, the Russian Museum is one of the two greatest repositories of Russian art.

96   The Rossi Pavilion in the Mikhailovsky Garden. 1819 — 23. Architect Carlo Rossi

97   The Mikhailovsky Palace (The Russian Museum)

98   The Museum of Ethnography. 1900 — 11. Architect Vasily Svinyin

99   The Mikhailovsky Palace from the Mikhailovsky Garden

96

97

98

99

100

101

100   The State Staircase in the Mikhailovsky
Palace

101 — 104   Rooms in the Russian Museum

102

103

104

**105   PORTRAIT OF COUNT FELIX SUMAROKOV-ELSTONE,
LATER PRINCE YUSUPOV. 1903**
By Valentin Serov
The Russian Museum

106

107

108

Nevsky Prospekt is the main thoroughfare of the city centre, extending for 4.5 kilometres. It begins close to the Admiralty and Palace Square and ends by the Monastery of St Alexander Nevsky. Nevsky Prospekt is made up today mainly of late nineteenth- and early twentieth-century apartment houses. Situated on this great avenue and nearby are palaces of the Russian aristocracy, cathedrals, museums, theatres and major shops.

106   The Yeliseyev shop. 1901 — 03. Architect Gavriil Baranovsky

107   The House of Books (formerly, the Singer Company building). 1902 — 04. Architect Pavel Suzor

108   The Alexandrinsky Theatre. 1828 — 32. Architect Carlo Rossi

109   Monument to Catherine the Great in the garden near the Alexandrinsky Theatre (1873, sculptors Matvei Chizhov and Alexander Opekushin)

110   Pavilion of the Anichkov Palace. 1817 — 18. Architect Carlo Rossi

111   The Moscow (Nicholas) Railway Terminal. 1851. Architect Konstantin Thon

112   The Trading Arcade (Gostiny Dvor), the Rusca Pavilion and the building of the former City Council (Duma)

109

110

111

112

113   A hall in the Shuvalov Palace

114, 115   The Sheremetev Palace. 1750 — 55.
Architects Savva Chevakinsky and Fiodor Argunov

116   The Bezborodko Dacha. 1773 — 77;
1783 — 84. Architect Carlo Rossi

115

116

117, 119 Interiors of the Beloselsky-Belozersky Palace

118 The Beloselsky-Belozersky Palace. 1846. Architect Andrei Stakenschneider

118

119

The early-nineteenth-century Yelagin Palace stands on a low rocky terrace, its main façade towards the park and its rear — with a hexastyle semi-rotunda in the centre — overlooking the Srednyaya Nevka River. Today the palace is used for exhibitions of applied art.

120 The Yelagin Palace. 1780; 1818 — 22. Architect Carlo Rossi

The Tauride Palace designed by Ivan Starov is an embodiment of the fundamental ideas of Russian Classicism. The austere simplicity of the façades contrasts with the opulent decoration of the halls. Today the building accommodates the Interparliamentary Assembly of the CIS states.

121 The Tauride Palace. 1783 — 89. Architect Ivan Starov

The Narva Triumphal Arch is a monument to Russia's victory over Napoleon. The name comes from the fact that at one time the city gate on the road to Narva stood on this site.

122 The Narva Triumphal Arch. 1827 — 34. Architect Vasily Stasov

127

Previous page:

123 Ensemble of the Cathedral of St Nicholas and the Epiphany. 1753 — 62. Architect Savva Chevakinsky

124 The Church of the Annunciation in the Alexandro-Nevskaya *Lavra* (Monastery of St Alexander Nevsky). 1717 — 25. Architect Domenico Trezzini

Designed by Rastrelli, the Smolny Convent Cathedral is a remarkable example of mid-eighteenth-century Russian architecture. The complexity of the façades, abundant sculpture and moulding, the placing of clustered columns on the projecting corners, and the highly ornate window surrounds are all typical features of the Russian Baroque. When Vladimir Stasov completed the building, he gave it a Classical interior.

125 The Smolny Cathedral. 1748 — 64. Architect Francesco Bartolommeo Rastrelli

The Alexandro-Nevskaya *Lavra*, a former monastery, was founded by Peter the Great in 1710 in honour of Prince Alexander Yaroslavich of Novgorod's victory over the Swedes in 1240. The remains of the canonized prince now lie in a silver shrine in the Trinity Cathedral here. Peter made the monastery the highest ranking in Russia. (The title *lavra* is reserved for the most important Orthodox monasteries.) The monastery is the location of the city's functioning Theological Academy.

126 The Alexandro-Nevskaya *Lavra*

Chevakinsky's Baroque-style Cathedral of St Nicholas and the Epiphany draws on the traditional forms of Russian church architecture. It was built on the former parade-ground of the Marines Regiment. Today St Nicholas's is the chief functioning cathedral in the city.

127 The Bell Tower of the Cathedral of St Nicholas and the Epiphany

128 The Cathedral of St Nicholas and the Epiphany

Overleaf:

129 View of the Smolny Convent

The Environs of Saint Petersburg

At the same time as the new capital was springing up, suburban residences for the Russian monarchs also began to appear. Within a period quite insignificant in historical terms, before the eighteenth century was out, St Petersburg became surrounded by a necklace of beautiful ensembles not only worthy of the capital but even echoing the various hues of its multicoloured brilliance. Triumphal and resplendent Peterhof; Tsarskoye Selo with its magnificent palace set in a park just made for meditative strolls; and Pavlovsk, where a smaller, yet still majestic palace is encircled by a rare variety of gardens, groves, alleys, bridges and paths. And in addition to these sparkling gems the necklace includes the estates at Oranienbaum, Strelna, Gatchina and more.

Peterhof is undoubtedly the most brilliant of the residences built outside the former capital, conceived with more than an eye to Versailles. Fountain jets, flanked by statues and mascarons glistening with gold, spurt upwards as if saluting the waves lapping the sea shore to which the alleys of the park descend. The exquisite palace towering over the park and the cascade of festive fountains was designed by the architect Rastrelli, the same man who built the Winter Palace in St Petersburg itself. The palace-and-park complex in Peterhof, though not very large, is so rich in artistic ingenuity, so generously endowed with light-hearted artifice, so refinedly simple, that it seems truly majestic in its inexhaustible variety. And the gloomy sea, visible nearly everywhere in Peterhof, provides an austere background to set off the glittering splendour of the palace, fountains and park.

Rastrelli also built the splendid Great (or Catherine) Palace in Tsarskoye Selo, with a façade extending more than three hundred metres. The regular French and landscaped English parks together with the finely proportioned pavilions which later appeared on the shores of the estate's lakes and ponds endowed this residence to the south of the capital with a special air of lyrical melancholy. It was here, at the Tsarskoye Selo Lyceum, that Alexander Pushkin studied at the beginning of the nineteenth century, here that he composed his first poetic works. And for Russians the wooded groves of Tsarskoye Selo have become an inseparable part of their cultural heritage, the Castalian spring of Russian literature, the dwelling of the national muses.

In its architecture Tsarskoye Selo represents the transition from the festiveness of the Baroque to the austere intimacy of Classicism which was to shape the character of perhaps the most surprising among St Petersburg's suburban attractions — Pavlovsk.

Situated no more than ten minutes' drive from Tsarskoye Selo, Pavlovsk already belongs to another era. The palace, an elegant and unpretentious creation of Charles Cameron which was extended and rebuilt several times, has retained both its severity of outline and an openness towards its surroundings. The park itself, laid out to the design of Cameron by Pietro Gonzaga and Vincenzo Brenna, is an exceptional piece of landscape gardening implemented in complete harmony with nature. Dark firs against a background of bright stands of birch, trees clustering on hilly slopes, stone pavilions set in amongst leafy boughs, statues made of bronze and marble, and romantic ruins in the spirit of Rousseau are all reflected in the waters of the winding Slavianka. The rare concord in which all these buildings, alleys, slopes and trees co-exist has made Pavlovsk a place with a special and unique charm. At a later time the concerts held in the famous Vauxhall (railway station building) where performers included the great Johann Strauss turned Pavlovsk into a musical centre of quite some importance.

In their appearance these park-and-garden complexes have kept the youth of St Petersburg alive, remaining untouched by the coarseness of the nineteenth-century "age of iron". Not only does one find in them a breath of unencumbered history, the chance to admire beautiful creations from the past, but time itself seems to have stood still amongst the sea, trees and rivers which even now remember Russia when it was young.

Mikhail Guerman

**130   PORTRAIT OF CATHERINE THE GREAT STROLLING
IN THE PARK AT TSARSKOYE SELO**
By Vladimir Borovikovsky
The Russian Museum

PETERHOF

The Peterhof ensemble is a magnificent monument of Russian architecture and landscape gardening of the eighteenth and first quarter of the nineteenth century.

Its heart, the Great Palace, was begun under Peter the Great in 1715, but subsequently rebuilt by Rastrelli.

Construction of the Lower Park on the shore of the Gulf of Finland started in 1710 with the general lay-out suggested by Peter himself. The natural rise on which the palace stands is adorned with terraces, two monumental flights of steps and the Great Cascade which is linked to the Sea Canal. The presence of the sea lends the park an enchantment all its own. The centrepiece of the Great Cascade, *Samson Rending Open the Jaws of a Lion*, symbolizes Russia's victory at Poltava in 1709, the decisive encounter of the Great Northern War.

131 Fountain: *Samson Rending Open the Jaws of a Lion*. 1801. Sculptor Mikhail Kozlovsky

132 The Great Samson (Sea) Canal and the fountain alley

133 The Great Palace (1745 — 55, architect Francesco Bartolommeo Rastrelli) and the Great Cascade

134 The Upper Park

131

132

135

PETERHOF

The Upper Park, inland from the Great Palace, is also adorned with pools and fountains. Peterhof's water-supply system, constructed in the early eighteenth century, is unique: unlike the fountains of European parks which were fed by machinery, here a natural difference in height from the source 22 kilometres away powers the whole magnificent display. The pressure is so great that the jet of *Samson* soars to a height of 22 metres.
The small Palace of Monplaisir was erected in 1714—24 in the Lower Park by Johann Braunstein and Jean-Baptiste Le Blond. Its interiors are lavishly decorated with ceiling paintings, stucco-work, lacquered panels, tiles and gilding. They now house a display of furniture, porcelain and other works of art typical of palaces in Peter the Great's time.

135, 136   The Neptune Fountain

137   The central parterre and sundial in the Upper Park

138   The Chessboard Hill or the Dragon Cascade. Dragon

139   Sea balustrade in front of the Monplaisir Palace

140   The Monplaisir Palace. The Bedroom of Peter the Great

141   The Monplaisir Palace. The Eastern Gallery

136

137

138

PETERHOF

Among the other architectural gems in the Lower Park is the Hermitage Pavilion designed by Braunstein and constructed in the 1720s. The last major stage in the evolution of the Peterhof ensemble was the creation of a third park adjoining the Lower Park on the East and called Alexandria after the wife of Nicholas I. Its most important feature is the Cottage Pavilion built by Adam Menelaws in 1829. Its appearance was strongly influenced by the Gothic style which was in vogue at the time.

142 The Monplaisir Palace. The Lacquer or Chinese Room

143 The Monplaisir Palace. The Central Hall. Sculptural group *Allegory of Winter*

144 The Cottage. The Drawing Room

145 The Hermitage Pavilion. The Dining Hall with the table laid

146 The Cottage. The Drawing Room. Mantel clock: *Rouen Cathedral*

147

148

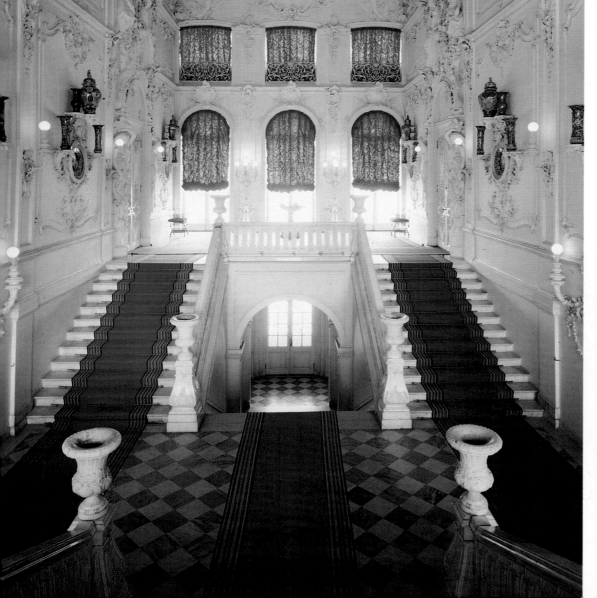

TSARSKOYE SELO

147   The Catherine Palace. 1752 — 56.
Architect Francesco Bartolommeo Rastrelli

148   The Catherine Palace. The Main
Staircase. 1860 — 61. Architect Ippolito
Monighetti. Originally designed by Charles
Cameron in the late 18th century

149   The Catherine Palace. The Central Gate.
Detail of the railing

150   Cupolas of the Catherine Palace Church

149

151

153

154

TSARSKOYE SELO

The Great (Catherine) Palace, a remarkable monument of Russian eighteenth-century culture, is the compositional centre of the architectural and park ensemble of Tsarskoye Selo. Among those who took part in its creation were many Russian architects, artists, sculptors and craftsmen. The palace was completed by Bartolommeo Rastrelli in 1752—56. Its façade, which is over 300 metres long, has a rich and varied décor. The parks of Tsarskoye Selo rank among the finest creations of Russian landscape gardening. They were laid out at about the time the Catherine Palace was being built.

Tsarskoye Selo is associated with the life and work of Alexander Pushkin who studied there at the Lyceum, and for some 50 years from 1937 the town has borne the poet's name. In the Catherine Park memories of Pushkin are evoked by the Lyceists' Walk and the sculpture *Young Girl with a Pitcher* by Pavel Sokolov, which inspired one of his poems.

The natural beauty of the park is enhanced by the Hermitage and Grotto pavilions, Marble Bridge and other architectural edifices.

155

156

157

158

159

160

161

162

ORANIENBAUM

161 Peter Bridge

162 The Great Palace. The Japanese Pavilion. 1710 — 25. Architects Giovanni Fontana and Gottfried Schädel

163 The Palace of Peter III. 1756 — 62. Architect Antonio Rinaldi

164 Stone Bridge over the U-shaped pond

165, 166 The Coasting Hill Pavilion. 1762 — 64. Architect Antonio Rinaldi. Originally there was a sloping track running from the pavilion down which people rode in special cars for amusement

167 Sculptural group *The Three Graces*

168 Entry Gate to the Peterstadt Fortress. 1756 — 62. Architect Antonio Rinaldi. The "Toy" Peterstadt Fortress was constructed for the future Emperor Peter III

163

164

165

169

170

171

172

ORANIENBAUM

The Upper Park ensemble of Oranienbaum consists of the Chinese Palace, the Palace of Peter III and the Coasting Hill Pavilion.
The Chinese Palace was designed by Antonio Rinaldi and built in 1762—68. Rinaldi's project was implemented by talented folk craftsmen — moulders, marblers, mosaicists and wood-carvers. The palace's ceilings were painted by well-known Italian masters of the Venetian academic school. Four Chinese Studies, decorated with lacquered panels, gave the palace its name. The palace's unique parquetry which was executed after Rinaldi's drawings by Russian craftsmen has survived to our day.
In the Palace of Peter III especially interesting are the stuccowork ornamentation of the ceilings and the lacquered panels of the doors.
The architectural gem of Oranienbaum is the Coasting Hill Pavilion, which blends harmoniously with the surrounding landscape.

173

174

175

176

GATCHINA

The history of the palace and park ensemble at Gatchina began in the 1760s when Catherine II gave the estate to Grigory Orlov who was the Empress's favourite and the organizer of the palace coup which brought her to the throne. The outstanding Italian architect Antonio Rinaldi was commissioned to draw up plans for a palace and construction began in 1766. Faced with stone, the palace blended harmoniously into its setting. Under its next owner – Emperor Paul – the palace was reconstructed (1796—98) by the architect Vincenzo Brenna. The greatest changes, however, took place not in the palace but in the park. In 1792 the estate was adorned by a Pavilion of Venus set on a small headland converted into an island and called the Island of Love. An important element in the park ensemble was Adrian Zakharov's Humpbacked Bridge, the only one in the park between two islands (the others connect islands to the lakeshore). The light golden colour of the limestone-faced bridge forms a striking contrast with the lush green banks of the Long Lake.

177, 179   Humpbacked Bridge

178   Landscape in the park

180   View of the Great Palace

181   The Venus Pavilion

182

183

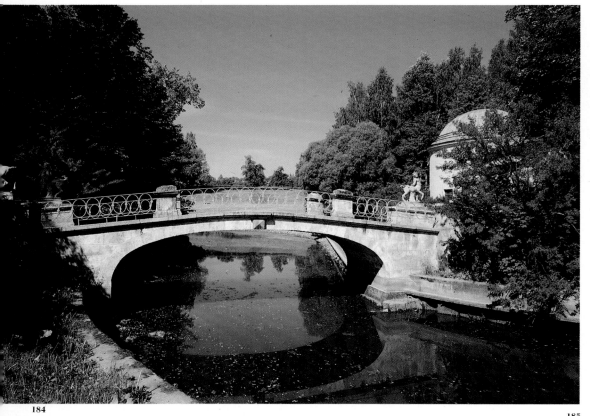

184

185

PAVLOVSK

The Pavlovsk Palace is an architectural monument of the late eighteenth and first quarter of the nineteenth century brought into being by the joint efforts of outstanding architects and sculptors. The museum has on display unique works of art. The collection of antique sculpture housed in the palace ranks among the richest in the country, second only to that of the Hermitage. The picture gallery boasts many canvases by well-known Western European artists of the seventeenth and eighteenth centuries. There is also a superb collection of tapestries and *objets d'art* in bronze, ivory and valuable minerals.

The Pavlovsk Park (600 hectares) was created by famous Russian architects over the course of fifty years, beginning from 1777. In spite of its long genesis, the park is compositionally an integral ensemble, its constituent elements fused together by an original artistic concept in one of the most beautiful landscape parks in the world.

186

192

193

194

PAVLOVSK

192 The Great Palace. The Picture Gallery

193 The Great Palace. The Greek Hall

194 The Great Palace. The Tapestry Room

195 The Great Palace. The Little Lantern Study. Oriel

PHOTOGRAPHS BY
VALENTIN BARANOVSKY, YURI BELINSKY, LEONID BOGDANOV,
KONSTANTIN AND NATALIA DOKA, SERGEI FALIN, GRIGORY KHATIN,
LEONARD KHEIFETS, ROMUALD KIRILLOV, FERDINAND KUZIUMOV, VICTOR SAVIK,
ANATOLY SIAGIN, VLADIMIR SOBOLEV AND KIRA ZHARINOVA,
AND VICTOR VASILYEV

INTRODUCED BY MIKHAIL GUERMAN

DESIGNED BY SERGEI DYACHENKO

TRANSLATED FROM THE RUSSIAN BY
PAUL WILLIAMS AND VALERY FATEYEV

EDITED BY
MARINA GRIGORYEVA AND IRINA KHARITONOVA

TO THE ORDER AND WITH THE ASSISTANCE OF THE *KOMETA*
PUBLISHING HOUSE AND *KOMETA-INVEST* INVESTMENT FUND.

САНКТ-ПЕТЕРБУРГ
Альбом (на английском языке)

Издательство «Аврора». Санкт-Петербург. 1994
Изд. № 2696
Пленки для цветной печати изготовлены
в МПО «Первая Образцовая типография»

Printed and bound in Belgium

С $\frac{4902020000\text{-}013}{023(01)\text{-}94}$ без объявления